Mother

Our Heavenly Connection

Mother
Our Heavenly Connection

George D. Durrant

Bookcraft
Salt Lake City, Utah

Library of Congress Catalog Card Number: 84-70437
ISBN 0-88494-523-5

2nd Paperback Printing, 1992

Lithographed in the United States of America

To Erma Gardiner
a marvelous mother of ten who told me to write this book
and to Jimmy Parker
who told me to write it with my heart and not my head
and to my daughter Kathryn
who helped me do it

Contents

Preface

Mothers can't all cook the same noodle soup. They aren't all equally patient. They aren't all firm in their discipline. They aren't all good at housework. They don't all have the same needs for fulfillment. They aren't all equally expressive of love. They aren't all thin and trim. They aren't all college educated.

Yet mothers are almost all alike in one important way. Each mother has the common yet uncommon role of being the primary influence on her children's destinies. That doesn't mean that each mother is responsible for her child's every action, either good or bad. Yet somehow the deepest part of a child's heart is shaped more by his mother than by all other sources combined. And if a mother's child can get some blessings from other sources as well, that child will be a fulfillment of his mother's dreams.

To have so profound an influence on the life of another is a most significant contribution. The reason we seek education—to become doctors, lawyers, or teachers—is to place ourselves in a position to have influence on the lives of others. Yet a mother relating to her child in the private intimacy of her home, with no audience but the unseen angels, is the predominant influence for all that is good and decent in the world.

Is it any wonder then, mothers, that our deepest feelings for you are those of gratitude? Thankfulness fills the hearts of us who are fathers because our children, who are dearer to us than life itself, are in your hands. We realize that we share equally with you the sacred responsibility of parenthood. But we also know that after we have done all that we can do, you make up the difference between what we can do and what needs to be done.

You mothers are the heart of the family's happiness. You are the source of influence that will lead us all to where we long to be.

May the Lord bless you with the physical, emotional, and spiritual strength to gently reach into the hearts of each of your children and give them direction throughout time and all eternity. May you ever be their connection with heaven.

An Open Letter to
Abraham Lincoln's Mother

No mother would think of herself as a model, but Sarah Bush Johnston Lincoln must have been an outstanding example in the role. Her wise encouragement and loving nurturing helped to bring to fruition one of the noblest characters of the nineteenth century.

1

Everybody's Mother

Dear Sarah Bush Lincoln,

You died over one hundred years ago, but you'll never really die. You live today because of the influence you had on your son Abraham Lincoln—and thus on the entire world. Knowing the kind of person that you were, I feel you would be interested in what happened in our home a few weeks ago.

We had just finished our evening meal. Paul, who married our daughter Kathryn, had left the table and was in the front room playing with their two small children. Mark and Sarah, my teenage son and daughter, had also finished eating and were in their rooms preparing for the evening's activities. Only Marilyn, mother of my children; Kathryn, mother of my grandchildren; and I were still seated at the round table in the kitchen.

As we talked about mothers I was reminded of the February 1945 *Reader's Digest* article written about you. It was titled "Abe Lincoln's Second Mother"; that would be you, wouldn't it, Sarah? Bernadine Bailey and Dorothy Walworth were the authors. I had read the article earlier and had been touched by what it said about you and your son Abe. I excused myself, got the article from my briefcase, and returned and sat down between these two wonderful mothers.

"Listen to this," I said with excitement in my voice. I then began to read about you. I had not completed the first page when my emotions welled up within me. Pausing after reading several paragraphs, I took a deep breath to regain my composure, then forged ahead.

Marilyn and Kathryn listened intently as I read how Tom Lincoln, whose wife had recently passed away, came from his wilderness farm in Indiana to Elizabethtown, Kentucky, to see you. He had left behind in the care of an eighteen-year-old cousin of his first wife his two children, Sarah, age twelve, and Abe, age ten.

At your small but fairly comfortable home in the security of a village settlement, Tom asked you, a girl he had known since childhood, to become his wife. Your husband had died three years earlier and you had three children of your own. You must have been a bit surprised by this sudden proposal, but you accepted. You packed your belongings and set out with your young ones and Tom for the unknown. You must have been quite a woman to do that, Sarah.

I'm sure you wondered what you were getting into as you rode in the wagon down the jolting, rutted roads. Finally you were aboard a ferry crossing the half-frozen Ohio River. I tried to visualize you in my mind and suddenly I was able to do so. Your eyes, your hair, your stature were exactly like those of my own mother.

The next several paragraphs were more difficult to read as I considered the greatness of your sacrifice and magnitude of your challenge. I paused, put my hand over my mouth, cleared my throat, and continued. I read of your arrival at the humble, one-room log home. Then, for the first time in your life, you saw young Abe.

You saw that he was as thin as a scarecrow and wore a ragged shirt and tattered deerskin pants. But it was the look in his eyes that got to you, although you couldn't have described that look. You got down from the wagon, took him in your arms, and held him close. You then said in a motherly tone, "I reckon we'll be good friends. Howdy, Abe Lincoln."

Suddenly, in my mind I was Abe Lincoln. I remembered the times when my own mother had come home. I remembered how she used to look at me, how she would hold me in her arms. I was so glad Abe had a mom again. I knew from personal experience that you can get by in life without a lot of things, but it's sure hard to get by without a mom.

I know you were at that time Tom's new wife, and I know he needed you. But much more than that, you were Abe's new mother. You entered the disappointingly ill-equipped and poorly furnished home. You must have expected better, but there was no time for self-pity.

My emotions settled somewhat as I read of how you took over and did what only a mother could see needed to be done. You asked Tom to get some wood for a fire so that you could boil some water. You changed the beds, including young Abe's, from dry leaves to feather mattresses, pillows, and blankets. You made clothes. You cooked stew. You made the small log house into a home—a home with a mom.

As I read on, my memories of my own mother placed me in Abe's place, so that for a time you became my mother. You did so many of the same kinds of things for your son that my mom did for me. That made me really love you.

Then my most tender emotions were stirred as I read: "Those first weeks Sarah felt mighty anxious. Especially about Abe, though he did what she said and never answered her back. Once she saw him looking at her real serious when she was putting some johnnycake into the oven. 'All my life I'm goin' to like johnnycake best,' he said suddenly, and then scooted through the door."

I really don't know what johnnycake is, Sarah. But I know what it was like to see my mom cooking scones for me. Do you know what they are? I know that looking at her in a certain way and having her look back at me the same way meant more to me than all the words and all the things in the world. As you know, Sarah, there is something that can pass between a mother and her child that is a more powerful influence for good than all the words ever expressed by tongue or pen. Such experiences write words upon the heart that can never be erased.

Marilyn and Kathryn could sense that the story I was reading was much more to me than a story of the past. I think they knew that to hear a story of a mother means more to a child than it does to a mother. No mother can really ever know what she means to her child. Only the child can know that.

I read on. The authors described how young Abe's jovial, fun-loving nature often got him in some trouble with his father. You would defend him, saying, "Abe's got a right to his own jokes." You sensed that Abe was somebody special who didn't belong to you but was yours to keep for a while.

Abe wanted to study for hours on end. His father thought that was folly, and would complain when Abe would read late at night by the fire. You would reply, "Leave the boy be." When he'd fall asleep reading you would gently cover him with a quilt.

Again I thought of my own life, remembering how I wanted to study art and how my dad thought that was folly. My mom would stand up for me too, Sarah. I don't mean to say that I was like your son Abe Lincoln in greatness—what I mean is, he was a boy and I was a boy. He had you for a mother to help him along, and I had my mom.

When your husband Tom and the others had gone to bed, you and Abe would stay up by the fire. He would read to you what he had written. When I read about his reading to you like that, my heart was again touched. I recalled how my mom and I use to talk about the things I had written. I wrote a theme once when I was in the eleventh grade. There had been a thicket of trees on Allens' property just beyond our barnyard. One day a bulldozer came in and knocked all those trees down. I was hurt because through the years I had played and prayed in those trees. I wrote about that. I read my essay to my mother and she cried. She told me I would someday be a writer. That meant more to me than anything my teachers had ever said.

Abe would read to you and ask, "Did I make it plain?" My eyes filled with tears as I read of your response: "It made her real proud when he asked her about his writing, and she answered him as well as anybody could who didn't know how to read or write."

I knew again what I'd known before, that it isn't what mothers know about things that matters. What matters is what they know about their children. You didn't know how to read or write, but you surely did know about Abe. Somehow you had a brief glimpse of his destiny and you knew with a motherly instinct how to influence him toward that destiny. The way you made him physically comfortable was important, but what you did for his soul was profound.

Finally, your boy Abe became Abe the man. Everything you could do for him, you had done. You gave him confidence in himself; you taught him he could be somebody. From you he learned, perhaps for the first time in his life, what it felt like to be loved.

As I read of his moving away from home, I remembered when I first left my boyhood home. At first, he came back often to see you. Later he could only come twice a year. On those special times the two of you would talk. He'd tell you about his law cases, about his work in the state legislature, and about his wife, Mary Todd. Even though Abe was not with you as often as he wanted to be, your influence never left him.

I remembered how after my mission I'd go to visit my mom. I'd stop in and tell her about my studies, about Marilyn, about the children. Mom liked to listen to me. When I left her to go on my way, I always felt renewed. Somehow all the influence she'd had on me was remembered. I wanted to make her proud.

As I neared the end of that article about you and your son Abe, each word meant more to me. All you had done for Abe, you had really done for all mankind. When he was in the public eye, in a sense it was really you. When you found out that Abe was going to Charleston for his fourth debate with Stephen A. Douglas, you went there too, without letting him know. You just wanted to watch him. In the crowd on the street you watched the parade go by. On a large float drawn by oxen there were three men splitting rails, and the big sign read, "Honest Abe, the Rail Splitter, the Ox Driver, the Giant Killer." Then he came, riding in an elegant carriage and tipping his tall black hat to acknowledge the applause of the crowd. You tried to shrink out of sight, but he saw you. He had the driver stop the carriage, then he got out and came over to you. He put his arms around you and kissed you.

The last time you saw him, he looked tired. In the way that only a mother and a child can, the two of you sat silently and communicated. He kissed you good-bye and said he'd see you soon. But you knew this was your final time together. When I read of that kiss I put my hand up to my forehead and covered my eyes. I remembered kissing my mother good-bye for the final time.

Oh, how I loved your son Abraham Lincoln at that moment! But far beyond that love was that which I felt for you, Sarah Bush Lincoln, his mother. In that quiet cabin in the wilderness of Indiana you had —without an audience, without fanfare, without worldly praise or recognition— made a boy into a man: a man who changed the world.

But what if Abe Lincoln hadn't become president? What if he had just been an ordinary man—a man who loved to read and write, a man who was honest, a man who always longed to come home and see his mother, a man who worked at an ordinary job and who loved his wife and children. You would have still done what you did, and there would be an unseen monument there by the banks of Little Pigeon River in Indiana. This monument would be to you—a woman who became a mother, who cooked johnnycake for a hungry, gangly boy, who softened his bed, who covered him with warm blankets, who encouraged him, who listened to him read . . . and who through her influence shaped his destiny.

Is it any wonder that historians now feel that when Abraham Lincoln said, "All that I am I owe to my angel mother," he was talking about you—his wonderful stepmother.

Sarah, your story taught me again that love between mothers and their children never changes. Different actors at different times act out their lives to the same story and the same plot. You taught us all that nothing a woman can ever do will have anywhere near as much importance as the influence she has as a mother.

Sincerely, one of your
millions of admirers,

George

An Open Letter to My Mother

The story of a mother means more to a child than it does to a mother. No mother can really know what she means to her child. Only her child can know that.

2

A Homemade Sissy

Dear Mom,

I really think I could have been a tough guy. You could have guaranteed that if you had spent more time with other people and less time with me. I wanted to be tough. You knew that, but you wanted me to be what we called in American Fork a "sissy."

You were always interfering in my life. You said that I was a good boy, yet at the same time you acted as if the world would come to an end if I didn't go to church. If I was so good, why couldn't you bear to see me miss church a few times? After all, church is a place to learn to be good, and you seemed to feel I was already good.

You were a soft woman, Mom. You weren't tough at all. I could get away with anything with you, as long as what I wanted to do was good. But let me try to do something tough, like I sometimes wanted to, and I could see a hurt look in your eyes. I couldn't stand to see that. Because of that kind of interference, I had to turn back to being a sissy.

Then there was that navy blue suit. It was all right to send for your dresses that were pictured in the Montgomery Ward catalog, but you really blocked me away from my tough-guy goals when you sent off to Denver for that double-breasted, navy blue suit.

I remember when it came. We unpacked it and I went in my bedroom and put it on. It fit perfectly, and when I came out I could see by the look in your eyes that I really looked good. I had a tie that you tied for me. Each week after church you told me to loosen the tie and pull it over my head so it would stay tied. That double-breasted suit wouldn't have done so much to keep me being a sissy except for the fact that even way back then I looked so good in navy blue.

When I'd pass the sacrament you would watch every move that I made. I could tell you wanted to stand up and shout, "See that boy right there, passing the sacrament, the one in the navy blue suit? That's my son. That's my George." If you hadn't been so reverent you'd have done that, wouldn't you, Mom?

Don't get me wrong. I didn't really mind the attention that you gave me. But was it really that big a thrill to have me dressed in my navy blue suit performing an errand for the Lord? Wouldn't some sort of public recognition for me or for you have been more fulfilling than that which we both privately felt in the chapel? Mom, don't cry, I was just asking.

People visiting in our home said, "Marinda, you sure do spoil that boy." I didn't know then what that really meant. Now, looking back, I know they were right. You really did spoil me. I think it was all part of your plan to keep me from being a tough guy. Nobody in history was ever as good to anyone else as you were to me. See-ing you, being near you, talking to you, was the center of all my happiness. My greatest boyhood fear was that I would lose you. So much of what I did that was good I did be-cause I wanted to please you. So much of my regret came from the times I knew I had disappointed you.

I've seen people influencing other people, but none of what I've seen has ever equaled the influence you had on me. You didn't take any psychology classes at college and you didn't read any books on the problems faced by teenagers, but you knew what was going on. Didn't you, Mom?

You knew that I wanted to be student-body president, and how I secretly and deeply regretted that I was never nominated. You knew how difficult it was for me to just barely make the basketball team. I was the little brother of Kent, who was a famous basketball star. I wanted so much to be like him, yet I felt so inferior. You knew I was shy around girls and insecure about my social life. You never said that you knew any of these things, but you did things that showed me that you knew. You must have known, otherwise why did you always do so much to try to build me up? You would tell me I was special. Did you really think that I was special, or that maybe someday I could be?

Did you really think the themes that I wrote for my high-school English class were good? I remember how you'd read every one and tell me that someday I'd be a writer. You never made a big issue about poor spelling, although you were a perfect speller.

You knew what you wanted me to be, didn't you? You always made me feel like you thought I was as perfect as all the other sissies in town. Why didn't you say more about my spelling errors and my other errors in other things? Why did you over-look so many of the problems I had in the here and now, and keep gazing off into the unknown future?

Or was the future really unknown to you, Mom?

If you hadn't been home so much I could have been tougher because then I could have faced up to problems on my own. Take, for instance, the December afternoon so many years ago when I was a high-school senior. I remember that cold afternoon as if it were yesterday. I came home from school and you were there. You were almost always there. You didn't need to be there; I could have made it on my own. But you were there. We had a basketball game that night with Ogden. When I came in and took off my coat, you told me to sit down at our big round table. "I'll cook you a pregame meal." You said it as if I were the one the entire team depended on to be the star.

I was really discouraged that day because I knew I wouldn't get to play at all. You started to fry me a huge pork chop and some potatoes. You kept talking to me about the neighbors and about my married brothers and sisters. I only half listened because I was wishing things could be different for me.

Finally the food was all cooked and you set it before me as if you were serving an all-American. Then you sat down and put your hands together and bowed your head and waited for me to pray. I would have prayed a lot less if you hadn't acted as if nothing good could happen if we didn't ask

God for it to happen. I prayed a short prayer. You could sense I was discouraged. You asked me what was wrong. I replied that it didn't make much sense to eat a pre-game meal for a bunch of strength and energy when you knew that all you were going to do was sit on the bench. You didn't reply. You just listened. It seems like you liked to talk a lot, but when you and I were alone in the kitchen, as we were so often, you always just wanted to listen.

An hour or so later, when I left to catch the team bus for Ogden, you came over for your kiss on the cheek. You always wanted your kiss on the cheek, didn't you, Mom? It didn't matter to you that tough guys didn't kiss their moms good-bye every time they set foot out of the house. Because of you I got so I couldn't bear to go anywhere without you having your kiss. I'm not sure now if it was you or me who really needed those parting kisses.

The last words that you said that day as I pulled my toboggan hat over my ears were, "You'll do good." I didn't really want to believe you, but I knew I would do well even if I did spend the game on the bench.

Just think, Mom, if you'd been out in the world somewhere on that cold day, you could have given a whole flock of people the courage and encouragement that you gave me. Of course, I liked the way things were in our quiet kitchen, with nobody looking on. Just you and me, Mom. I needed you more than the million others who could have had your influence.

You surely did have a hold on me, Mom. You made it so I never wanted to run away from home. Instead, I always wanted to run home. I'd get homesick just being at school from eight to three. I'd come home, you'd be there—although there were some times when I wondered which came first, me or a Relief Society quilting bee.

You loved to make quilts, didn't you, Mom? You'd put up the long boards in our front room and stretch some cloth on them. Nine or ten ladies would come and you'd all go to work. On those days, when I'd come home from school, you'd shout out a hello. But, much to my despair, I'd have to make my own peanut-butter sandwich.

One afternoon you were in there quilting away and I could hear a lot of unorganized talk. You ladies liked to talk almost as much as Dad and the men down at Chipman's store. Anyway, the general subject that day was the theory that the young people in the town were going to the dogs. They were, according to the talk, worse than any other young generation had ever been.

One by one the ladies took turns describing the misbehaviors that were occurring at the high school. I noticed that you were unusually silent throughout this one-sided debate. Finally your voice rose above the regular volume and caused all the others to become silent. I could hear you through the half-closed door. I can still recall every word of your great speech. You said: "I don't know if the kids at the school are doing all that you say they are. All I know is that my son George does not do those things."

You didn't close your talk in the usual "Amen" style, but nonetheless you had just given the most meaningful sermon I had ever heard. Silently, and unknown to you, I pledged to quit doing those things.

Yes, Mom, I have millions of memories. I still feel the gentle hammering of your motherly strokes on my head and on my heart, shaping, ever shaping my every thought and deed.

I guess the truth is that I was a sissy from birth. I tried to hold that kind of behavior back, but your whole goal seemed to be to bring it out. I want so much to be what you want me to be—and once in a while, for a fleeting moment, I am. At those times I am what you, with your gentle influence, have made me.

I am and hope I can forever be a home-made sissy.

3

You Will Be There

I saw you last when I said good-bye as I was about to depart to serve as mission president in Kentucky and Tennessee. You remember the day of that good-bye. You were in failing health when I was asked to serve. The circumstances surrounding our lives at the time this call came were very different from those some twenty years before, when as a young man I had been called to serve in England.

The earlier call had prompted some questions as to whether or not our family circumstances and finances would enable me to leave. The bishop came to our home and asked if I could go. As our family and

Bishop Grant sat somberly in the parlor, Dad said, "George can't go. I'm ill; I can't care for the chickens; we will have no money. He can't go." I remember the hurt look that came to your face, Mom, as you sat up straight in your chair and through your tears said, "Bishop Grant, Bert is ill. I know he can't take care of the chickens. But I'm still strong. I can feed them and gather the eggs. I can do the work. We can make it and my son George can go." And so I did.

Remember how proud you were of me as, dressed in a new navy blue suit that you had purchased for me at Devey's men's store, I stood and gave my farewell address. You wanted me to go, but I sensed that both you and Dad realized how much you would miss me. I was your youngest; when I departed all the children would be gone.

Until that time, the only times I had ever been away from you were for three days at the Mutual Dell Camp, three days in Salt Lake City at the Newhouse Hotel for the State Class B Basketball Tournament, and five days at a time at National Guard training at Camp Williams. I didn't know if

I could bear being away from you for two years—two years seemed that day to be the same as forever.

We drove to Salt Lake City and arrived at the Union Pacific Railroad station. We didn't say much, you and I. Dad didn't either. Finally the last minutes were gone. There was only time for one more thing— one thing that rose in importance beyond any other word or deed that had ever been spoken or performed. I put my hands on your shoulders, leaned forward, and kissed you on the cheek. A surge of comfort in my soul told me that it would not be for the last time.

We wrote often, didn't we, Mom?

You did gather the eggs and feed the chickens. My older brother John helped you and cleaned out the coops. As you entered the chicken coops three or more times a day, the chickens caught the vision. They wondered at first where I was. When they realized I was on a mission and you, Mom, were working to support me, they decided to do their part. They laid more eggs than any chickens we'd ever had before. You worked harder than a mom should ever work. The Lord blessed us. The money came and I had what I needed.

I wasn't the best Elder in the Church. But I was always doing my best all the while I was in England because I knew what you were doing to keep me there.

Those were wonderful days, weren't they, Mom? I was telling the missionaries and Saints in England about my mom, and you were at Relief Society showing the sisters my picture and saying, "See, here is George; doesn't he look handsome? He is a missionary in England, you know."

But now it was twenty years later. This second mission call was different. You were ill. Dad was gone and you were lonely. You looked forward each week to having Marilyn and me and our eight children come down from Salt Lake City to visit you. With this mission call you knew that those visits would end.

Finally, the time for our departure was just days away. We came to the old family home for our last visit. Our talk together was not as lighthearted as our talks usually were. The dark cloud of separation loomed heavily over our hearts. We ate and did our best to forget what was soon to be. Finally it was time for the good-byes. One by one Matt, Kathryn, Devin, Marinda, Dwight, Warren, Sarah, and Mark hugged and kissed you, their grandmother. One by one they went out the front door and ran toward the waiting car. Finally you stood up and Marilyn embraced you and tearfully said good-bye.

Then it was just you, Mom, and me. We were alone in the spacious kitchen as we had been so many times before. The kitchen where you'd made me peanut-butter sandwiches, homemade noodles, hot biscuits, and one special pork chop. The room where I had kissed you on the cheek at least seven thousand times. You were standing near the old rocking chair by the window where I would sit so many years before on the few occasions when you'd be away. I'd watch the headlights of each car coming up the Alpine road, hoping that they would be the lights of the car that would bring you home to me.

You were weeping openly and I inwardly. I walked closer to you. I felt as if my heart would break and I knew that yours already had. I reached out to put my hands on your shoulders as I had done so many times before. You put your arms around me and held me tighter than I could ever remember.

You begged me not to go.

I didn't want to leave you, and yet we both knew that it was in my going that we would some time be together forever. I pulled away, and as I did, you became calm. I looked deep into your tear-filled eyes. I expressed my everlasting love. I bent forward and for the last time I kissed you on the cheek.

Five months later while in Kentucky I received a phone call from Duane that your tender but tired heart had been stilled. I went to my room and knelt in prayer. My heart rejoiced. Now I knew you would grieve no more. It was then that I felt your presence. You came to me. You were there. You saw our beautiful mission home.

A few days later you got in the car with me and we headed down the winding roads of Kentucky and Tennessee. You saw the green fields, the white fences, the southern mansions. You met all the missionaries. I could tell that you were proud when each of them called me President. I could tell that, even though the missionaries couldn't see or hear you, you wanted to shout out, "This man that you call President—this man in the navy blue suit—he's my son." Then you turned away and went to your new home.

You really were proud of all us kids, weren't you, Mom? All you really seemed to want was our happiness and success. Perhaps you wanted more. We all want things that others don't know we want.

Someday, somewhere, we will have it all. You will be there, Mom, and if I continue to make you proud of me, I'll be there too. We'll have millions of memories, won't we, Mom? One more thing, Mom—if you bend down I'll kiss you on the cheek because I'll love you forever.

Your devoted son,

George

An Open Letter to Marilyn, Our Children's Mother

My fondest wish for our children has been that they could have from their mother the same gentle and powerful influence that I felt from mine. And my wish has come true.

4

Our Leading Lady

Dear Marilyn,

When I fell in love with you, Mom voluntarily and of necessity walked away from her role as my leading lady. From that time on you became the co-star of my life—my eternal partner and the mother of my children. There is not, nor can there ever be, anything that I could have provided for our children that can equal, even in a small way, that which I did for them by arranging for you to be their mother.

I discovered in our early days of courtship and marriage the many virtuous qualities of your soul. These qualities, I knew, would make you a glorious mother. My fondest wish for our children has been that they could have from their mother the same gentle and powerful influence that I felt from mine. And my wish has come true.

You, Marilyn, and my mother were not cut from the same piece of cloth. No two mothers are. You and she came to motherhood at different times and on different roads. My mother's procedures and techniques for filling her role as a mother were different from yours. Who can say that a good mother must fit a certain pattern in all that she does?

As I've told you, Marilyn, my mother's influence was of the soft kind. She thought I was the most handsome young man in all of American Fork. I'd get dressed up in my orange knit tie, my brown tweed sports coat, my pink shirt, and green trousers. She'd look at me and say, "You sure do look nice."

You were different, Marilyn. Even before we got married you started telling me if the clothes that I wore did or did not look wonderful. You also informed me when you felt the things I said and did were either good or bad. It was shocking at first to learn that I wasn't perfect. But after a while I became rather accustomed to the straightforward manner in which you treated me.

Yes, you were a bit more realistic than Mom had been. You even declared that you felt that I wasn't really all that handsome. "George," you said, "you aren't pretty and you aren't homely." Then before I could discern exactly what you meant, you added, "You are sort of in between. You are pretty homely."

I knew then that when our children came they would get a more accurate reflection of truth from you than I ever received from my mom. And of course I realized you had a keen sense of humor and were just joking. You were just joking about my looks, weren't you, Marilyn?

Up until I met you, I had been accustomed to having my mother fuss over me and attend to my every need. She seemed to thoroughly enjoy making me delicious peanut-butter sandwiches. When I asked you to provide me with such a treat your reply was, "Why don't you make it yourself? Have you got a broken arm?" I knew then that my children would learn more about self-sufficiency in the kitchen than I had ever learned.

I remember telling you one day, "You surely are different from Mom." You abruptly replied, "That's because I'm not your mom." I knew then that my children would get straight and rather blunt answers from their mom—the sort of answers that I had never received in my American Fork home.

Shortly after we were married, I gave a talk in church wherein I was a little wishy-washy on a certain point of my testimony. As we rode home you expressed your disappointment in what I had said. I felt terrible and wondered how you could be so critical of the one you claimed to love. We didn't say much more about your comments or about anything else that night. But in my silence I decided that the next time I'd show you. I decided I'd never be wishy-washy again.

I knew then that my children might have plenty of faults, but that if you, their mother, had your way they wouldn't be guilty of being wishy-washy.

I remember that after we were married we knelt down for our evening prayers. Before we began you said, "We have each been missionaries. While we were with our companions on our missions we'd bear our testimony to one another before we prayed." You suggested that you and I were now companions and should do the same. We did, and have continued to do so through the years. It has brought a marvelous influence into our home.

After that sacred suggestion I knew that our children would never have cause to wonder about their mother's love and loyalty to the Lord.

In those early, prechildren days, I was majoring in art at Brigham Young University. In my sculpturing class, I had an assignment to create a figure out of a large piece of wood. I set my heart on carving something from a log. We had no car at the time, and so I couldn't really get to the woods to get such a log. I walked around the neighborhood in hopes that I'd find one in someone's yard.

It was on a day when I was feeling a little sorry for myself anyway. You know how I get feeling like that sometimes. I felt frustrated that I didn't have a log. Then I decided the reason I couldn't get a log was because we didn't have a car. I concluded that the reason we didn't have a car was because we didn't have any money. "Why do we have to be so poor?" I asked myself.

I decided to lie down on the bed and feel sorry for myself. You asked me what was wrong. I gave my usual answer, "Nothing." You persisted. Finally I said, "I need a log to carve for my sculpture class. And we don't have a car so I can't get one so I guess I'll fail the class and fail college and fail everything else in life."

Instead of giving me the sympathy I thought I needed, you put on your coat and walked out on me. A half hour later you opened the front door and entered, dragging a log behind you. You never told me then or since where you got that log. It was

really a beauty—the very log I had en-
visioned in my mind that I needed.

When you laid it at my feet I was completely choked with emotion. I wanted to
reach out and pull you close and tell you of
my love. So often I want to do that because
of what you do for me. But so often I don't
seem to be able to say or convey to you
how deeply grateful I am to you. I try—but
words just won't do it.

I took the log to the art class. I began to
chip away the outer bark and finally the
wood itself. I carved almost unconsciously.
Finally, a figure of a woman emerged from
wood. The teacher came to me, and as we
both backed away to have a general look,
he put his hand on my shoulder and surprised me by saying, "George, you have
carved the exact image of your wife."

It was then that I realized that my heart
and not my head had directed my hands. I
had indeed followed an inward pattern of
my love, and the final product was you.

That experience was symbolic of my
deepest feelings about you. I knew then that

when our children were frustrated and discouraged, you wouldn't sit around and feel sorry for them. You'd find them a log and encourage them to carve out their own destiny.

I also knew that our children, by following the thoughts put into their hearts by you, would carve out of their lives the exact and everlasting image of you—their mother.

The stage was now set. The rehearsals were over. It was time for the really big show. It was time for the children. As one by one they entered the stage I knew that each would have scenes in which only he and you would be on stage. Quiet, private scenes in the kitchen, in the bedroom, in the car, and walking along the way. Scenes where the only audience would be the unseen angels. Scenes where the child would be influenced by your sense of humor. Scenes where the truth would flow from mother to child in a firm and loving manner. Scenes where a child would learn to make his own peanut-butter sandwiches. Scenes where a young one would learn never to be wishy-washy. Scenes where your clear and bold testimony of the Lord would be transfused from you to the child. Scenes where you'd give him a log and then stand by as a model while he did his own carving.

The houselights would soon dim, the curtain would soon come up, and our children would be born and take their places as the stars of our show. I looked forward to seeing your influence on them, my dear Marilyn. I wanted them to be like you. I dreamed of them growing up possessing the same qualities of character and spirit that you possess.

I was glad that you and I would often be on stage together. I was grateful that, on those occasions when only a mother could be on stage, it would be you. I was glad that you would forever be our family's leading lady.

5

The Difficult Years

We were married many years ago on an icy cold winter's day in mid-January. Recently, in speaking of that day, you jokingly said, "I'd never do that again."

"Sure you would," I replied.

"Don't be too sure," was your response.

"Look at where we are in life. We've had some real successes. And look at our children. Don't you think it has all been worth it?"

"Oh, sure, when you look at what we've done and our children. Then I know it's been a wonderful life. But we've sure had some hard times along the way. At least I have felt they were hard times."

I could tell that you were in a reflective mood, and as I thought back through the years, I sensed that at times life is indeed difficult, especially for a wife and mother. In an effort to show understanding I softly said, "You always amazed me at how you did what you did. I saw you get discouraged, I heard you cry, I saw you weakened by physical strain. I saw your worried concern but I never saw you give up. You never turned away. You always turned toward the center of things and walked directly into the action. You have been a tough woman, Marilyn."

I smiled as I added, "You told me once that if the man had to give birth to every other child, the largest number of children in any family would be three."

I remember a letter you wrote to me when our family was younger. In it you wrote: "George, you just don't realize how difficult things are for me. I know that you try, but there are so many things that you don't understand because you don't experience them. With Matt, Kathryn, Devin, Marinda, and Dwight still so young, and as

I near the time of the birth of our new baby, I sometimes wonder if it is all worth it. Sometimes with all the demands on me and the physical and emotional strain involved, I wonder if I can make it.

"You are busy in your work and in your church assignments and you are so proud of our little family that you can't quite see that I need more of your help and love. Most of all, I need your understanding.

"I can tell that sometimes when you come home from work you are a little disgusted that the house is a little cluttered. I sense that you wonder what I've been doing all day.

"I snap at the children for some little thing they do wrong and you look at me like I am a tyrant. I feel like a tyrant. I don't want to be ornery with you and them. It's just that at times I feel like a failure as a wife and a mother and even as a human being."

You closed the letter by appealing to me that we sit down and talk about things. I remember that as we talked it seemed to help. I got the feeling that the best way I could help you during those difficult years was to be with you and talk to you. Yet so often I reacted in just the opposite way.

I remember the time in Brigham City when the children cried most of the night. Because I had a very important meeting early the next morning in Salt Lake City, I felt I'd better get a good night's rest. So when the children would wake up I'd remain in bed while you attended to their needs. After all, I reasoned, all you had to do the next day was stay home with the children.

When morning came I slipped quietly out of bed so as not to wake you or the children. I began to get dressed and discovered that I did not have a white shirt that was ironed. As I plugged in the iron to try to iron only those parts of the shirt that would show under my coat, I wondered, "What does Marilyn do all day?"

As I began to prepare my own breakfast I discovered there was no bread. I felt a slight twinge of disgust as I wondered, "How could she forget something as important as buying or baking a loaf of bread?" I hurriedly made hot cakes. I love hot cakes and I didn't have time to follow the recipe. "I know what goes in hot cakes," I said to myself as I cracked an egg into a cup of milk. Soon I was ready to eat. I took the first bite and was repulsed at the taste of what I had created.

By now my disgust was fully mature. I wanted you to know that I was completely displeased with your performance. Usually the best way I could do that was to be silent and not speak to you. On those occasions you'd sense I was upset and ask, "What is wrong?" I'd reply with an unpleasant, "Nothing is wrong," and again become silent. But, with you not there to observe my disgusted silence, all the negative emotion I was feeling was being wasted.

It was then that I decided that silence wouldn't work. I decided to bang around. The best time to bang around—move a chair, throw pans in a cupboard, and so on —is in the silence of early morning. I was sure that if I banged around, you would wake up and say to yourself, "George is banging around. I must have done something wrong."

Finally, when it was time to leave, I came back into the bedroom. I got my suit coat from the closet and put it on. Then I decided that if I really slid the sliding door hard, it would make the loudest bang of all. You'd really know then that I was upset.

I slid the door. Bang! Now you'd know. To cinch my message I'd leave the bedroom and the house without saying good-bye. Then you'd really know that I was upset and that you needed to do better as a wife and mother.

In that mental state I went to my office to get some papers for my meeting in Salt Lake. Because of the journey and the importance of the meeting I knelt to pray. As I did so, all I could think of was you. I said, "Heavenly Father, please bless Marilyn that she will have a happy day!" Then it seemed that I heard a voice say, "George, you go back home and bless her yourself—you are much closer than I am."

I ran back to my car and drove the few blocks back home. By now you were out of bed. Something had awakened you earlier. It took courage for me to do it, but I said,

"Marilyn, I'm sorry." Then I said something that was easier to say after what I'd just said. I added, "And I love you." I gave you a kiss and as I went out the door I shouted back, "I sure hope you have a happy day."

I relate that story to you now because it is symbolic of so much of our lives during the difficult years when our children were young. You had so much to do and needed my understanding, and yet at times I was caught up in my own needs and often failed to reach out and help you.

I remember that when we did sit down to talk you explained: "I feel bad that at times I get discouraged. It's just that on top of other things we have so many bills and that worries me. Our car is always breaking down and we can't afford any luxuries. I want to talk to you about these things more than we do, but I can tell that all that does is discourage you. I don't want to add any burdens to you because I know that you're doing your best. You need a cheerful, energetic wife. But at the same time, I need to be so many things that are difficult for me to be." You continued: "I see other women who apparently are far happier than me. Their homes seem neater, their clothes nicer, their interests more varied. At times I wonder if we are really going the right way, and if my sacrifices are worth it."

As I heard these remarks I must have looked quite sober, for you said: "But there are bright spots, and I really would not trade places with anyone in the world. I am always proud of you and I am grateful that you try so hard to be a good man and a good father. The children are cute because they look like my side of the family. They are good most of the time, and I am deeply grateful to be their mother. When we take them to church and other places, I'm proud to have them all there. Family home evenings are a joy to me because you do the teaching."

I smiled and felt better as you continued: "Family prayer helps. And dreaming about what the children can become brings sunshine into my heart. I feel that each of the children is special. It's hard for me not to brag. That's why I like to visit your mother. I can sit and brag to her about you, her son, and about our children, her grandchildren.

She is probably the only one I can tell the truth to without worrying about people thinking I am boasting about my family."

Yes, those days that came and went so quickly were difficult but critical years for you and for me and for the children. You did far more than your share to pull us through.

I remember how we all needed you and how you always came through. I recall an experience we had while I worked for the Indian Seminary Department at Brigham City. I made a decision there about the time of day the Indian students should come to seminary. I felt that it was a sound and wise decision. My leaders in the head office felt that I had erred in judgment. They came to Brigham City and kindly criticized me. I wanted so much to be successful, to be known as a good teacher and a wise administrator. Feeling that my leaders had lost confidence in me pained my soul and caused me to doubt my own self-worth.

I didn't want to go home and tell you what had happened. I couldn't disappoint you. Yet I didn't know where else to go or whom else to tell. When I came home you were alone in the kitchen. The children were in the backyard.

I blurted out, "Marilyn, I've got some bad news." Then, with tear-filled eyes, I told you the story. When I finished I said, "So, Marilyn, my career is shot. I'm not going anywhere; you married a failure."

We looked deep into each other's eyes. You reached out and took my hand in yours and said, "George, I didn't marry a failure. Your career is not ruined. You are the greatest man that ever lived and I love you with all my heart."

Your voice was like the voice of an angel —all my doubts were swept away. I was a new man. I knew then what I've known so many times, that all that mattered to me was what you thought of me. Oh, how I needed you then and so many other times! You never have let me down—and what you have been to me you have also been to the children. You've carried your own heavy burden and yet you've had the strength to carry much of the load for each of us. Now, thinking back, I wonder how you did it. Strength that you scarcely could muster was needed to cook our meals, bathe the children, wipe their noses, change their diapers, read them books, sing them songs, help them with school work.

You didn't resent your duties, you only wanted me to understand that you were trying. You wanted to see in my eyes that I could appreciate what you did rather than criticize what time and sometimes energy would not allow you to do.

You only wanted me to take my turn with home duties. You knew that when I came home at night I had worked all day and was tired. You just wanted me to know that you had worked all day, too. Instead of criticizing the cluttered house, I should have pitched in to clean things up. You didn't want me to help grudgingly, but willingly and with understanding. You wanted me to cheerfully care for the children while you went visiting teaching, to evening Relief Society preparation meetings, or to your much-loved genealogy class. You never wanted to back out of your lot; you just wanted me to be supportive of the most difficult of all tasks—that of being a mother.

I tried to help, but still you were pretty well on your own. When we would talk—and as I said, we didn't do that enough—you would tell me of your frustrations and of your joys. I remember when you told me of certain Relief Society lessons that meant so much to you because they focused light on the purpose of life and the nobility of motherhood. Another time you told me of your discussions with a sister in the ward with whom you went visiting teaching. You loved her because her life-style was similar to yours. You wouldn't tell me the complete content of such discussions because you said that sometimes you told her of my inadequacies and she spoke in the same way of her husband. But then you added that most of the time the two of you took turns bragging about the marvelous men to whom you were married.

You told me of some of the women you knew who were really struggling, torn by the conflicts between gospel principles and the philosophies of the world. These women were, as Elijah said, "halting between two opinions"; they were not comfortable with what they learned at church, nor could they fully embrace the things they were hearing from other sources.

You tearfully explained to me how grateful you were to base your goals upon divine and never-changing truths. You testified to me that you knew that each of our children had come to us from God. You expressed your deep desire to influence your children to do good. As we talked I was impressed with the insights and strength that were growing in your soul and that seemed to be nourished by the difficulties you were facing. I was grateful that my children had you for their connection with heaven.

I remember saying to you, "I suppose Mom had her difficult years." "I'm sure she did," you replied, adding, "I believe many women do, especially those who want to be good mothers. Now, as the older children are raised and the youngest ones are getting alarmingly close to leaving home, the rewards completely outweigh the burdens. Now, at times, I'm so proud I can hardly refrain from running to the phone to call my sister Sharon to tell her what Matt, or Kathryn, or Devin, or Marinda, or one of the others has done. Even when I am called upon in church to speak, I want to spend the whole time talking about my family. And that is what I'd do, except you tell me not to."

Now whenever you speak of your family you beam and almost glow. Has it all been worth it—I mean, considering the difficult years and all? I can hear your proud reply, "What do you think?"

I remember recently when one of our married children came in the house and asked, "Mom, could you tend my children for an hour?" You replied, "I sure can't—I'm off to teach my calligraphy class." (You're the best calligrapher in all of Salt Lake, in my opinion.) You picked up your supplies and hurried out the door. Your most difficult years are behind you, and you are willing to let your daughter endure her difficult years because you know the rewards of motherhood.

The fact is, you want for your daughters what you had for yourself. That is, I suppose, the best answer to the question, "Would you, my dear Marilyn, do it all over again?"

6

What You Want Them to Become

Now that the children are all grown out of their diapers and the most difficult years are fading into sweet memories, we have some glorious times as a family whenever we are together.

All in all, we do a lot of laughing. It makes up for the tears you used to shed in the difficult years. We like to sit around on those times when all the children come home and talk and laugh. Almost all of our conversations are about "the olden days" when the children were growing up. When we talk it seems as though during those days we were all in heaven without even having died.

Almost every time we talk the conver-
sation turns to the subject, "Mom was
harder on me than she was on you." The
older children band together to prove that
you were more strict with them than with
the younger ones. The younger ones attack
back, telling stories to prove that the older
ones got away with far more than they do.
Finally all seven gang up on young Mark,
the baby, and each provides evidence that
Mark is spoiled and gets away with things
that would have brought upon them the
wrath that only you, their mother, could
bestow. As the conversations become more
pointed, Mark moves closer to your side,
and that causes me to remember having
done the same in a similar but earlier cir-
cumstance.

Every year that passes, the children's
minds form bigger stones with which to
build monuments to their mother. Every
time we talk the monumental stones become
more numerous. Stones that were once
small incidents between a mother and a
child have now become family legends.

Matt, who at this time is in his last year
of law school at Harvard, leads the way in

his "mother stories." He has always been a talker and a thinker and thus an excellent arguer. He would argue with you on every subject and at every turn. You couldn't always win with logic, but you could get him with your inspired bits of wisdom and with your humor.

At our family gatherings Matt tells story after story about you. Once he said: "Mom has said things to me she would never say to you others. Once when I was just twelve years old we sold our station wagon and bought a little two-seated car. We were out for our first family ride, a trip to Grandma's place in American Fork. I pointed out several times as we passed through Orem that it was a mistake to have purchased such a small car for such a large family. I complained about being crowded all the way from Provo to Pleasant Grove. Then Mom had the audacity to say in a loud voice, 'Matt, this car wouldn't be too small for our family if you didn't have such a big mouth.' " Amid tumultuous family laughter Matt confided, "I was crushed. Mom never said anything like that to any of you." Marilyn, who is consistent, said, "None of the others had a big mouth like you did." Matt reeled like a bear who had just been hit by an arrow. "See, she said it again!" he shouted with the pride that comes from proving a point.

Matt, who was unwilling to yield the floor to the other seven children and their similarly moving "mother stories," continued: "When we lived in Kentucky there was a huge tornado that swept its way through the city of Louisville. I was a senior in high school. My friend and I followed along in his car right behind the tornado. Later we drove around for two hours looking at the damage and trying to find a road heading home that was not blocked by fallen trees. Finally we arrived at my friend's house. His parents were frantic and ran out to greet us, shouting to my friend and crying, "Oh, our dear son, we were so worried. We wondered if we would ever see you again." Matt described dramatically how the worried and relieved parents allowed their tears to flow freely as they embraced their son.

Continuing, Matt said: "I then departed and ran home to reassure Mom that I too was all right. I threw the door open and shouted, 'Mom, it's me, Matt; I'm safe, I'm home.' Mom was over in front of the TV and just barely looked around to see me. All she said was, 'Hi, Matt, I'm listening to this report about the damage.' I couldn't believe it. I told Mom about the different and much more appropriate greeting my friend's parents had given him when he came home. I guess that really got to Mom, because she stood up and turned toward me and replied, 'Matt, I wasn't worried about you. I've been around you enough to know that you are a far bigger wind than that tornado.' " At that moment I could feel the pride in Matt's tone as he felt he had proved that Mom was harder on him than she had ever been on any of the others.

I took the floor for just a moment and said: "I know that your mom worried about you children. But until she had heard that the worst had happened, she didn't sit around worrying that the worst was about to happen. You have had a calm mother. Her sense of humor helped with that. Many moms aren't calm. They get pretty nervous about a lot of things. That's all right—it's hard to get over being nervous if you have a tendency in that direction. Nervous mothers produce good children, but it's more fun to live in a family where the mom is more funny than she is nervous.

"Your mom didn't humor you, but with her sense of humor she's taught you life's most valuable lessons. Her humor has done much to lubricate the friction that could have so easily arisen in our home.

"Of course, she's also done a lot of crying. God gave mothers the talent both to laugh and to cry. She wouldn't have been such a good mother if she hadn't known how to cry. She couldn't have reached her full depth of influence unless she wanted happiness for you children so much that any reverses would make tears fall."

My comments made us all feel a little more serious than we usually do. After a few seconds of silence, Devin and Kathryn added their stories about how you had made them do their best, had gotten after them for doing wishy-washy things, had made them work in the house and in the yard. All you would reply was: "Sure, it's all true. All you say is true. The things that I did were exactly the things you kids needed. Your dad was sometimes too soft on you, so I gave you what you needed."

I knew what you said was true. I was so proud of you. I told the children, "Your mom has that rare talent of being hard and loving at the same time." Because so much of the talk at family gatherings centers on you rather than me, I could feel slighted. But I could never be jealous of you, because you and I are one. Our children are the pride of my life. If you hadn't been the way you are, the children wouldn't be what they have become.

You are the one who had the difficult years. You're the one who suffered most, worried most, spent endless hours on the private stage of our home watching small but eternally significant dramas that no one but you and the angels ever saw. You're the one who paid the price. You're the one who worked your miracles at home.

You're the one who convinced Matt to go on a mission, he says. He told me that he wasn't sure if he should go even though I, his father, was at the time a mission president. His talent for intellectualism caused him to wonder. He felt that without a firm testimony he could not sincerely serve. You are the one who sat on the bed beside him and reasoned with him. At that same hour I, his father, was traveling many miles in another direction in order to give a talk that would bring me public acclaim but would not influence anyone to the degree you were influencing Matt.

You told him alone in the still of the night that he should go on a mission. You explained to him how your testimony had come as you had served, and how his would also develop. He did not argue with you at that time, for he knew you were right. You helped him know what he should do. You knelt and prayed at his side and his spirit was strengthened.

You see things as being either black or white. You aren't wishy-washy. You are willing to discuss things that seem gray to others, but not until you establish the right side. You answer requests for things and favors with a quick "no," but then you compassionately consider any reasonable appeal to turn the "no" to a "yes."

So, at family gatherings, stories continue to flow about you. Each child tries to top the others' stories of what Mom refused to allow him to do. I remember another instance when Matt led the way. "When I was a junior in high school," he remembered, "almost every kid in my class went from Kentucky to Florida on spring break, but you wouldn't let me go."

You replied: "I didn't stop you from going. All I said was that I didn't feel good about you going and I thought the whole idea was unwise."

"Yeah," Matt replied. "How could I go after that?"

"You didn't want to go anyway. You knew it wasn't a good idea."

Matt soberly replied, "Yeah, I did know I was better off not to go. It was at a time in my life when if I'd gone I could have gone down the wrong path."

I often wonder if, even after his graduation from Harvard, Matt will ever be able to win a case against his mom.

Devin finally got center stage, which is hard for him to do at home. He has a lot of fame outside the family because of his athletic ability, but at home he is just "one of the eight."

"Yeah, Mom," he said, "I was trying to decide where to go to college. I had a lot of schools inviting me to attend. It was a tough decision for me. Then one night, about three in the morning, for some reason I awoke. I looked up and there you were, standing by my bed in your white nightgown. When you saw I was awake you said, 'Devin, you don't need to think about it anymore. You are to go to BYU.' Then you turned and departed. I wasn't sure whether I had just seen the angel Moroni or my mother. Either way, the next day I told BYU I was coming."

The other children seemed amazed at this story, and one asked, "Did you really do that, Mom?" You replied, "Of course I did. I never let any of you make a decision without telling you how I felt about it. I thought he should go to BYU, so that's what I told him."

You'll remember that Warren didn't volunteer to tell his almost sacred experience, so I asked, "Warren, can I tell them what your mother did for you?"

"Sure, if you want to," he replied. And I told them the story you know so well.

One day when I came home from work you told me that you, Warren, who was a high school senior at the time, and I were going to have TV dinners up Millcreek Canyon. I was shocked because in my many years as a father we had never had TV dinners up Millcreek Canyon. You continued, "Warren has something to tell you and we need to be alone, just us three."

What has Warren done? I wondered. *He's a good kid, but he must be in serious trouble.* I imagined several horrible things and prepared myself for the worst one. As we drove the five miles to a picnic area no one spoke a word. Finally, at the foot of the mountains, surrounded by pine trees and with the gurgle of a clear stream nearby providing the background music, we had our blessing on the food. As we silently began to eat, you bluntly announced, "Warren has something to say and you listen to him and try to understand."

Warren gulped and then looked across the picnic table into my eyes. "I'm not playing football," he said softly. "And not only that—I'm not playing basketball when that comes, either."

I couldn't believe what I was hearing. All my brothers had participated in high-school athletics; all my sons had played. It was what Durrants did. And here was my son telling me he wasn't going to play. I knew he had made a mistake. I was sure that I could convince him of the value of playing. He'd quickly understand so that he could repent, we could eat our chicken, and we would all go home happy.

I calmly started my rebuttal to his proposal. You stopped me by saying: "Warren and I have talked about this all afternoon. He didn't want to talk to you because he knew you wouldn't understand and would try to talk him out of it. So now you just listen."

Warren continued: "I'm not as good at basketball as my brother. Everybody expects me to play because of him. I don't like to play for the school. I just want to play on my own for the fun of it. I don't need the fans, the coaches, or the pressure. There are other things I can do better than my brother or you. I want to do those things. I want to be myself, not someone else."

I could hear him but I couldn't understand him. "Don't be a quitter, son," I said passionately.

You sternly interrupted, "He isn't a quitter—he just wants to do the things *he* wants to do."

"Don't you want him to play?" I asked. Then, before you could reply, I added, "I know you are always bragging about Devin."

"I'm proud of Devin," you replied. "But this isn't Devin here at the table; this is Warren. Warren is a wonderful son. He doesn't have to be a Devin. He has never quit anything that is good for him and for us."

After that we silently swallowed our food. We cleaned up the table, and you and Warren walked close together as we headed for the car. I was hurt. I looked up at the sky that was turning dark enough to show its stars. I looked at you, Marilyn, and I understood. As we loaded the garbage into the trunk of the car I looked into Warren's eyes and asked, "Warren, are you willing to have the courage to tell your coaches of your decision?"

"Yes, I am," he replied.

"What will your friends say?"

"My real friends will understand."

As I looked at Warren I knew I was looking at a man, not a boy—a man who had courage of the highest degree. I was filled with a feeling of respect for him. You, his mother, had on this occasion stood at his side. Some of your courage had flowed into him and given him the extra strength that he needed.

This had not been a wishy-washy encounter. It had been straightforward, and I've never seen a more dramatic expression of love come from a mother to a son. You had insisted that Warren choose his own log to carve. All you wanted was for him to carve the log to the best of his ability.

Telling that story caused me to realize that so much of what our children are has come from you. So much has come in the nights, when as children they cried. So much has come as they sat near your side —so much on the afternoons when they came home from school and told you their feelings.

Then Kathryn spoke up and, in a more quiet way, said: "Because we moved a lot, I had my share of inward insecurities. My patriarchal blessing indicated I should go to my parents for advice. I had a hard time doing that. For a time I drew away from you, Mom.

"Finally I was out of high school and left for Provo to be on my own. I was there for almost a month and had grown a little more homesick than I had supposed I would. One night I had a date with a special young man. During the course of the evening he told me he was uncertain about serving a mission. When I pressed him to learn why, he indicated that he had great difficulty reading. He was embarrassed to announce that he had never read the Book of Mormon or any of the scriptures because he could not. I wanted to help him so badly but I didn't know what to say.

"When I entered my apartment I knelt

to pray, to ask the Lord how I could help this humble friend. I had an impression that I should call you. I dialed the number with some reluctance because I knew you would be in bed asleep. After several rings I heard you say, 'Hello.' It was like finally getting through to an angel in heaven.

"I told you about the young man and asked you what I should do. In a calm and loving manner you gave me several suggestions. We talked for a long time. Finally I said something that I had held back for several years. I told you, 'I love you, Mom.' Your reply was, 'I love you, too.' "

And the monument to you grows ever larger. It's no wonder you like to go to the phone to call Helen Moon and say, "Hi, Helen, guess what Mark did today," or "Marinda is getting married to the greatest guy in the world," or "Dwight had an amazing experience on his mission," or "You should have heard what Mark's teacher said about him." Then Helen takes her turn to tell you of her wonderful children.

The payoffs are really something, aren't they, Marilyn? It's getting so that if you and

Helen Moon reported all the good things your children did, the two of you wouldn't ever get anything else done except bragging.

I remember one night when the children were younger. We were all gathered in our front room for family home evening. We'd have one person in the family be the target and then the rest of us would take turns saying good things about that person.

Finally it was your turn. Each of the children said some nice things about you. Just before I was to speak, ten-year-old Matt said, "Dad, if I said all the good things I know about Mom, we'd be here all night." His sincere words touched my heart. I confirmed his words by saying, "Kids, I feel the same way about your mom that you've all said you do. I love her with all my heart. The best thing I could have ever done for you children was to give you such a marvelous mother."

I love you, Marilyn,

George

An Open Letter to My Seventeen-Year-Old Daughter, Sarah

We might be last in accepting the social changes prescribed by world opinions, but what does the Bible say about being last? "The last shall be first." We will forever be first in the joy and happiness that comes from families.

7

A Bright Future

Dear Sarah,

This is the second letter in this book addressed to a Sarah. The first was to Abraham Lincoln's mother, Sarah Bush Lincoln. This one is to you, my seventeen-year-old daughter Sarah.

The last few days I've been reading a book about the future. The author predicts the changes he feels will occur in our social structure within the next twenty years—the very years in which you will become a mature woman, a wife, and a mother. No woman will have ever come to her "best years" in more exciting times than you.

Marriage in your day, the author says, will be less and less a lifetime commitment. Partners will marry their first mates for excitement and romance. Following divorce they will marry again, this time for companionship. Then, as they tire of this relationship, they will divorce and perhaps marry again. The author bases this prediction about divorce on the belief that as the human life span increases, married couples will not be able to endure such a long period of time with any one marriage partner.

Those who wish will be able to obtain a yet-to-be-developed drug that will double their life span. To get the drug, a person will have to agree to have only one child—a replacement for him or her. How does all that sound to you, Sarah? That will be quite a world, won't it?

These social changes will flourish first on both the east and west coasts of the United States, and will sweep inland to all the states. Guess where the author says these changes will come last, Sarah. That's right—it is predicted that the last state to accept social change of this sort will be Utah. Why is that, Sarah?

It isn't living in Utah that will make us last, it is our religious beliefs. How does it make you feel when brilliant people such as the author of such a dynamic book state that we will be the last ones to really get with the times? Does it make you feel a little bit ashamed, or does it make you feel an inward pride?

During the next several years you'll hear much about changing values in our world. Professors, television personalities, newspaper articles, books, and so-called enlightened friends will advise you to come into the modern world. The wind of social change, which in the past has been but a breeze, has now become a full gale and in the future will become a hurricane.

Some people will be like sailboats drifting with the wind. They will call out to you that they have never been so free and so fulfilled. Others will want both to drift freely and to hold an anchor that can be thrown out if needed to hold them to certain old values. There will be a few who will sink their anchors deep enough that they will be able to hold on to that which should never change.

Oh, my dear Sarah, sink your anchor deep and hold on to eternal values. Don't let prevailing winds of the world determine the waters in which your life's ship will sail. Realize that, although we have feelings and beliefs that we know to be true, others have feelings and beliefs that are directly opposed to ours. They are equally convinced that they are right.

Discussions on the role of women and the place of motherhood are rewarding if they are conducted in a spirit of love and an honest search for understanding. But when such discussions become arguments, they are as futile as the debate once held over the relative merits of the sun and the moon. The debater arguing for the moon won with the argument that the moon shone at night when it was needed, while the sun only shone in the daytime, when it was light anyway.

Many have no anchor to divine truths. They feel that whatever they think is best for them at a given time is the right thing. Those who do not believe that God has prescribed any one way will, of course, come to different answers than those of us who do believe in a right path.

We believe that we lived as spirits before we were born as mortals. Others don't believe that at all. We believe we have been given commandments by a loving God. Others don't believe that. We believe that the role of being parents is a sacred trust from God, and that our main priority in life is the family. Others feel that family is important, but no more so than any of their other desires. We could make a much longer list of how we are different from others. We aren't always better than others, but we are different.

So, what does all this mean to you, Sarah? The answer is, of course, up to you. But I, your father, have some advice for you.

As time goes by, you will get even more beautiful than you are now. If any boy falls in love with you while you are in high school, tell him in a friendly way to go jump in the lake. Tell him to jump in a shallow place where he can get to shore, because you may be interested in him again in a few years.

Then, after high school, go on to college or to a technical school. While doing so, date and let feelings of romance take their natural course. But don't sit around and act as though getting married and becoming a mother is the only future for which you need to plan. Plan a career that you could pursue if you didn't ever get married or if marriage was delayed for a while. Some girls don't plan on any future other than marriage. When that doesn't come, as it sometimes doesn't, they do not have the satisfaction that comes from being really good at something they love to do, something at which they can earn a good living.

But if romance and then marriage does come, plunge into that with all your heart. Get married in the temple. The commitments that you make in the Lord's house will anchor your ship in a harbor of happiness.

If you can, after marriage, keep going to school to get your full education. But if you and your husband can't both go to school, then fall back to the anchor of the gospel. Decide, in the light of all the truth you know, what would be best for you and for him and for the children.

During this decision-making time the winds of the world will blow into a tornado force. The rope that ties you to your anchor can be strained to its limits. If you decided to untie it for a time, you could be blown away to a place where it would be more difficult to find a new anchor.

If you or your husband or both of you are still in school, and the only way that can continue is not to have a child, what will you do, Sarah? Again you'll hear voices from without and from within. Your anchor will still be there. The two of you will make decisions that will determine the future waters in which you will sail. Will they be waters filled with family waves or personal waves, or a mixture of both? And if there is a mixture, be sure that family waves will be the ones that you love the most.

When a baby comes you will have three loves: your husband, the little one, and a career. All will tug at your inward desires.

What will you do, Sarah? Suppose you are a fashion designer and have just had some real success at work. Will you stay home with the baby or will you continue to work? The rope tied to the anchor will be strained.

If you go out of the home to work, you'll try to find a truly good woman to care for your baby. You'll want the best for your little one, because you'll be a great mother, Sarah. You'll find someone to tend the child who will love the child as you do. It will be hard to find someone like that, won't it? But you'll try.

Then, after work and on weekends you'll make up for the time away. You'll spend almost all your time with your husband and baby—because, as important as your career is, you'll never let it become more important than this little one.

Perhaps when the baby comes you'll decide to put your career aside for a few years. You would do that if you could afford to. But finances may be tight. You might suppose that if you don't continue to work you will not have the money for the many things you desire for your home. And per-

haps without your income the very neces-
sities will not be attainable.

If you are blessed, as are so many who
hold to the anchor, you'll be able to afford
to stay home and be a full-time mom, and
you'll want to. Oh, you'll miss your career
because you loved it and it made you feel
like a complete and worthwhile person. But
you'll have an even deeper desire to stay
home.

You'll enjoy the baby more than words
can describe. You'll help the little child feel
loved all the time, as only a mother can.
You'll hold her close. You'll teach her the
things that matter most—things about being
loved and feeling worthwhile. You'll become
aware, more than you've ever been before,
that the time when a child's future is most
determined is in the preschool years. You'll
learn that the mother's greatest influence
comes before the child learns to read or
write.

There will be days when you'll look out
of the window and see a gentle breeze blow
through the lilac bush. On those restless
days you'll long to be back at your career.

Sometimes you'll feel it a bit of a waste to be home when you could be out there. But you'll hold the baby close and feel more content and less unsettled.

Other babies will come. People will wonder why you want more than two. The winds of the world will blow messages of abortion and small family size. You'll push their voices aside, but perhaps you'll still wonder. Finances will be tight as the children come.

The pressures of managing a home and meeting the needs of the children and your husband will be strenuous. Finally the children will be in high school. Now they will need so many costly things. Then you'll know, as so many have learned, that children are expensive but they last a long time.

All through these years you'll be making decisions. Your choices will be influenced by the winds of the world or by the anchor of the gospel.

Perhaps when the children are a bit older you'll go back to your career. That way the money for college and missions will be more available. But your work will still be a second priority to your family.

Through the years you'll love your husband. Your career and his will not be measured against each other. He may well have less talent for earning a living than you will have. Love him, honor him, be at his side. He will need you and you will need him. Pray with him, pray for him, praise him, and sustain him in his role as father. Have him read this:

Dear son-in-law,

You surely are lucky that you found Sarah and won her love. I'm sure you would agree that she is really something. Take care of her. When you and she make the great decisions of life, make sure they are based on the divine anchor of truth that you and Sarah share. Make sure that what you decide will make her happy and fulfilled as a woman.

When children come, Sarah's strength will be taxed to the limit. Put your needs, as best as any of us can, second to hers. If both of you need to go out of the home to work, then both of you need to come home and do the housework. There isn't now, nor has there ever been, any part of gospel doctrine that says a man can't change diapers, wash dishes, or vacuum floors. And if you go out to work and she stays home, come home and help just as if she had also been outside the home at work. Above all, appreciate her efforts at home and do all within your power to see that she gets free time away from the children and away from home chores.

Encourage her to use her talents. Tend the children while she attends night classes. Hold the babies in priesthood meeting while she teaches Relief Society.

Try to understand her. That doesn't mean that you always will, but try. When she cries, try to bear up and do what you can to help her. She needs your emotional support and love more than she'll ever need anything else in the world.

Your greatest joy in life will be in seeing Sarah happy as your wife and the mother of your children. There is no greater experience for a man than to live with a happy wife.

God be with you and her always.

Love,

Father George

Now, Sarah, in closing let me say that I've observed that you have the talent to be whatever you desire to be. But among your greatest gifts from God is your ability to influence others.

I remember several years ago when you were going to elementary school. Late one afternoon the phone rang. I answered it; it was the elementary-school principal calling. His first words were, "I want to talk to you about your daughter Sarah." My heart quickened its pace as I wondered if you were in some kind of difficulty. He then added, "I don't usually call parents to talk to them as I wish to talk to you. Usually it's just for the opposite reason." My heartbeat was even more intense with that statement. Then he added, "I just want you to know the kind of influence your daughter Sarah has on this whole school. Because of her and the way she conducts herself and the things she does, every student in this school is a better person."

I was not quick with any reply, because of the gratitude I was feeling in my heart. He then concluded by saying, "I just wanted you to know that, Mr. Durrant. And I wanted to thank you for the influence your daughter has on us all."

While I was teaching at Brigham Young University, a girl from my class came to my office to talk to me privately. She asked me if I thought she could get into the movies. I said, "I think so, if you have enough money for a ticket." We both laughed because we knew her question was not about watching a movie but about being an actress. She had been in many productions at BYU, and was beautiful, and very talented.

As we spoke more seriously, I told her I thought she had an excellent chance of being an actress if that was what she wanted. She said, "But do you think if I was an actress I would be able to hold to the standards of the Church?"

I looked into her eyes and thought for a few seconds, and then felt impressed to say, "Oh, yes, you could."

Then tears came to her eyes and she could scarcely speak. Finally gaining her composure, she said, "I don't really want to be an actress. What I really want to be is a wife and a mother. But," she continued, "I'm scared. I have seen heartbreak in my own home and I was just wondering if it was possible to get married and be happy."

The spirit in the room was such that my eyes were moistened with tears also. I slowly said, "I want you to know it is possible to get married and be happier than you've ever even dreamed."

We then sat in silence for a few seconds, until she finally said, "That's what I wanted to know, Brother Durrant. My real goal in life is to get married and become a mother and be happy."

And so, Sarah, I say to you as I said to her, "It's possible to get married and become a mother and be happier than you've ever dreamed." I feel that those who will finally be born with you as their mother will be of all those born upon the earth the most fortunate—the children who will as infants lay close and feel the warmth of your body and your spirit, the preschoolers who will enjoy the fun-loving nature of an exuberant mother, the teenagers who will receive counsel from one who has studied the dating scene as intensely as you have, and the adult children who will be so grateful that their mother was Sarah. You have a glorious future!

In three earlier letters I spoke of Abraham Lincoln's mother and the influence she had on Abe, and of the influence my mother had on me. I described the way your mom helped shape your destiny. In your own way and in the most interesting of all times you, Sarah, will influence your children as those mothers influenced theirs.

Yes, the future will bring many changes, Sarah. But for you the future will be very kind, because you have an anchor. Along with being a wife, becoming a mother will be the fulfillment of your major dreams. God bless you, Sarah.

With my love,

Your Father